Engelbert Humperdinck

**Hänsel and Gretel**

A fairy opera in three acts

Engelbert Humperdinck

**Hänsel and Gretel**
*A fairy opera in three acts*

ISBN/EAN: 9783337245009

Printed in Europe, USA, Canada, Australia, Japan

Cover: Foto ©Thomas Meinert / pixelio.de

More available books at **www.hansebooks.com**

G. SCHIRMER'S COLLECTION OF OPERAS.

# HÄNSEL and GRETEL

## A FAIRY OPERA

IN THREE ACTS BY
ADELHEID WETTE

TRANSLATED AND ADAPTED INTO ENGLISH BY
CONSTANCE BACHE

THE MUSIC COMPOSED BY
E. HUMPERDINCK

COMPLETE VOCAL SCORE BY
R. KLEINMICHEL

G. SCHIRMER INC. NEW YORK.

# ARGUMENT

ONCE upon a time a poor broom-maker and his wife lived in a lonesome cottage in the Harz Mountains with their little son, Hänsel, and daughter, Gretel. When our story opens, the father and mother have gone away to sell brooms in the neighboring villages, leaving the children at work in the house. But work is tiresome, especially when empty stomachs are clamoring for unattainable goodies; finally the youthful pair start to romping about the room, and at the height of their frolic the mother enters, weary from her long trip and unhappy because she has been unable to sell her wares. She scolds the children, and sends them out into the forest to pick wild strawberries for supper.—Late that evening the father returns, having disposed of his brooms at a good profit, and gaily unpacks a quantity of dainties; then, missing the children, he asks after them, and is horror-stricken at thought of their pitiful plight all alone after nightfall in the woods.

Act II discovers the children roaming through the woods, gradually filling their baskets with strawberries; heedless of direction and time, eventide finds them bewildered in the darkening forest haunted, as they have been taught to believe, by fairies and witches. The steep, rocky bulk of the Ilsenstein, a reputed gathering-place for evil sprites, looms up amid the trees; the wind whispers and moans uncannily, and shadowy bush and hollow take on strange and fearful shapes. The frightened children cower together beneath a spreading tree, and repeat their usual bedtime prayer to the "fourteen guardian angels," after which, calmer in spirit, they fall asleep with a fairy vision of the radiant angels floating around them.

Act III opens at daybreak; the children awake, refreshed by a good night's sleep, and sing merrily. All at once they notice an object overlooked in the evening darkness—a beautiful little house built of all manner of good things to eat, and giving off a most appetizing odor. This is, alas! the abode of a wicked witch, an ogress who entraps small boys and girls by her spells, pops them into her oven, and bakes them into delectable gingerbread, upon which she fares. Hänsel and Gretel approach the house and begin to break off tasty morsels from the walls; the witch appears and in due course casts a spell over them to prevent their escape; she now shuts Hänsel up in a sort of cage and feeds him on sweets to fatten him; then she tries to entice Gretel to bend down in front of the oven, so that she may be able to push her in and bake her; but Gretel pretends not to understand, and when the witch herself crossly bends down to show her how, the two children quickly shove her into the oven, bang the door shut, and dance around gleefully. Thereupon, all the gingerbread shapes that formed the hedge around the witch's house are transformed—her spell being broken—into their rightful shapes of happy boys and girls who thank Hänsel and Gretel for their deliverance; then the father and mother, who have been seeking their dear ones, burst upon the scene, and all winds up with a chorus of thanksgiving.

# Hänsel and Gretel.
*Richard P. Condie - Director*

## Dramatis Personæ.

---

| | | |
|---|---|---|
| **Peter**, a broom-maker | *Douglas Merril* | Baritone. |
| **Gertrude**, his wife | *Alice Beth Whitley* | Mezzo-Soprano. |
| **Hänsel** } their children | *Ferris Edgley* | Mezzo-Soprano. |
| **Gretel** } | *Alice Carlson* | Soprano. |
| **The Witch** who eats children | *Mary McGregor* | Mezzo-Soprano. |
| **Sandman** (the sleep fairy) | *Barbara Perritt* | Soprano. |
| **Dewman** (the dawn fairy) | *Eulalia Condie* | Soprano. |
| **Children** | | Sopranos and Contraltos. |

Fourteen Angels .......................... *Ballet.*

---

First Act.        Home.
Second Act.    The forest.
Third Act.      The witch's house.

# Hänsel and Gretel.
## Prelude.

Ruhige, nicht zu langsame Bewegung.
Andante con moto. (♩= 69)

E. Humperdinck.

Copyright 1895 by B. Schott's Söhne.   31957

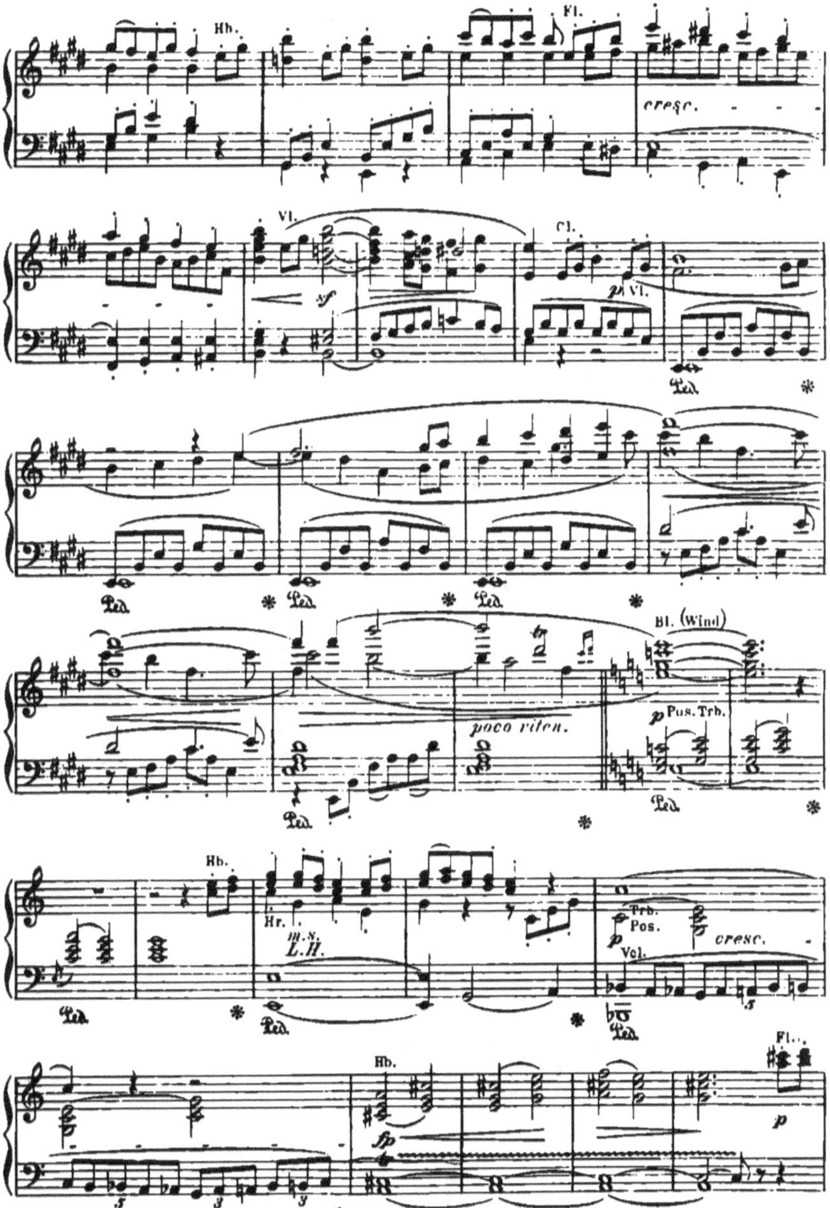
Hb.
Fl.
cresc.
Vl.
sf
Cl.
p Vl.
Ped.
poco riten.
Bl. (Wind)
p Pos. Trb.
Hb.
Hr. I.
m.s.
L.H.
Trb.
Pos.
p
Vcl.
cresc.
fp
Fl.
p

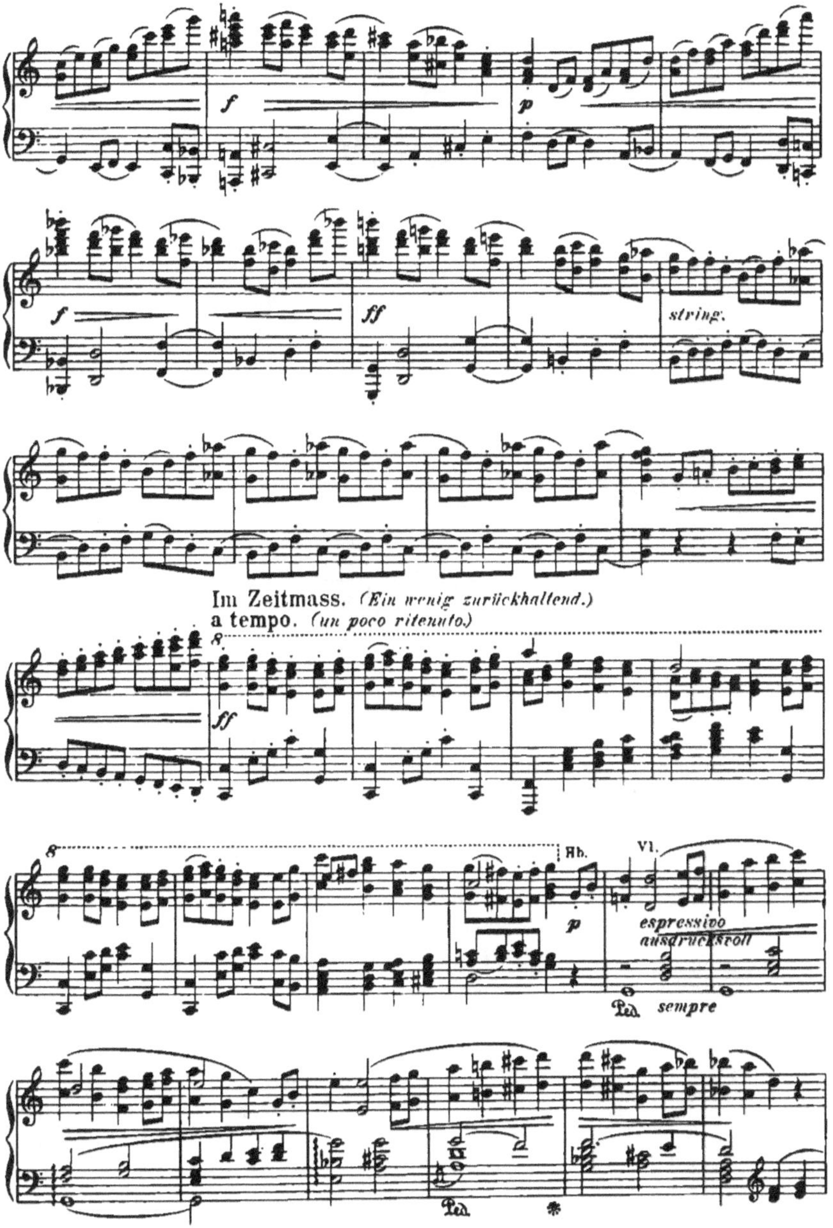
f
p
f
ff
string.
Im Zeitmass. (Ein wenig zurückhaltend.)
a tempo. (un poco ritenuto.)
ff
Hb.
Vl.
p
espressivo
ausdrucksvoll
Ped. sempre
Ped.

# First Act.

## Home.

Allegretto con moto. (♩. = 63)

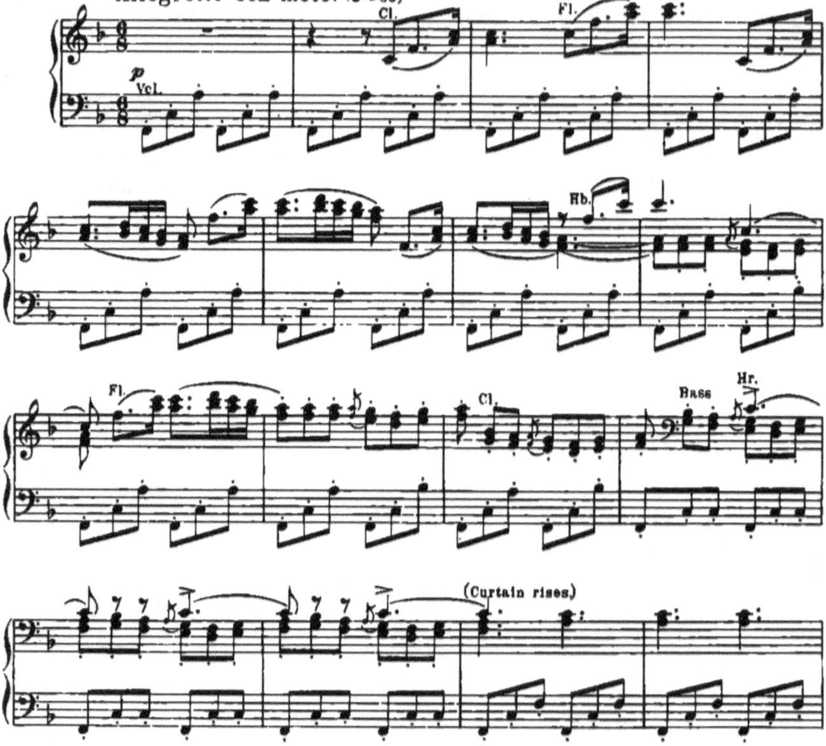
Cl.
Fl.
p
Vcl.
Hb.
Fl.
Cl.
Bass
Hr.
(Curtain rises)

### First Scene.

(A small and poorly furnished room. In the background a door; a small window near it, looking on to the forest. On the left a fireplace with chimney above it. On the walls are hanging brooms of various sizes. Hänsel is sitting by the door, making brooms, and Gretel opposite him by the fireplace, knitting a stocking.)

Gretel.
Su - sy, lit - tle Su - sy, pray what is the news?
Hb.

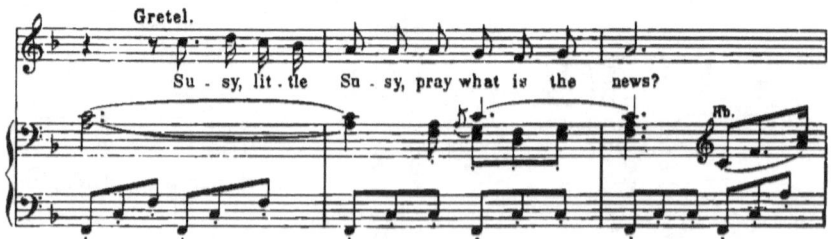

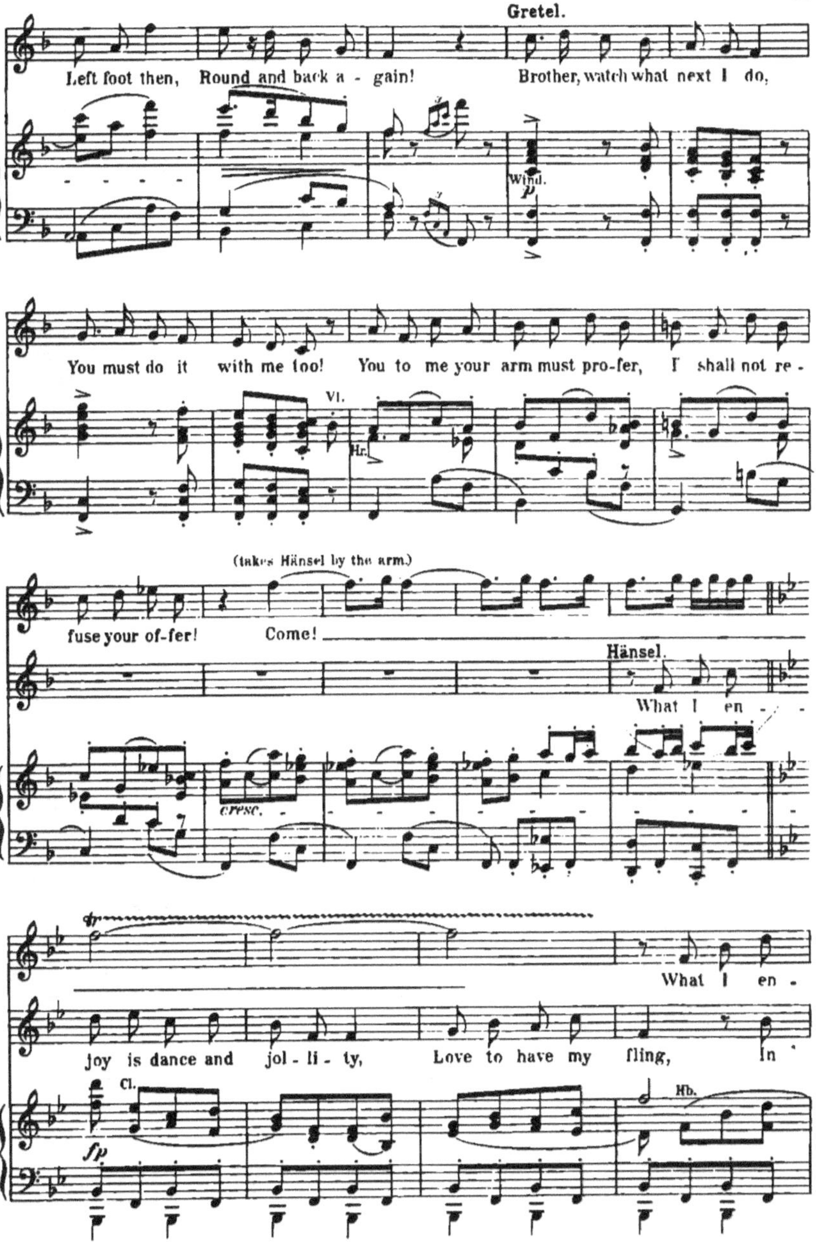
Gretel.
Left foot then, Round and back a - gain! Brother, watch what next I do,
Wind.
p
You must do it with me too! You to me your arm must pro-fer, I shall not re -
Vl.
Hr.
fuse your of-fer! Come!
(takes Hänsel by the arm.)
Hänsel.
What I en - -
cresc.
What I en -
joy is dance and jol - li - ty, Love to have my fling, In
Cl.
fp
Hb.

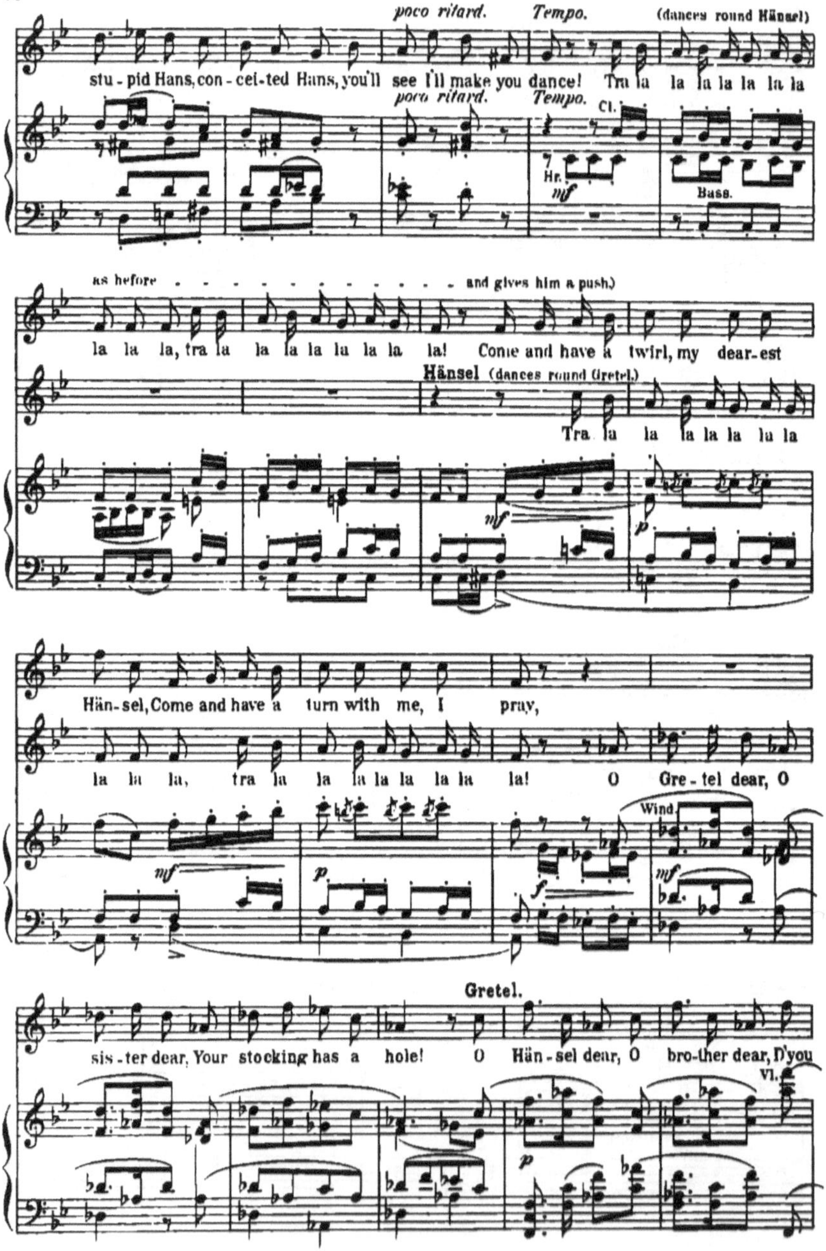

*stu-pid Hans, con-cei-ted Hans, you'll see I'll make you dance! Tra la la la la la la la la la, tra la la la la lu la la la! Come and have a twirl, my dear-est Hän-sel, Come and have a turn with me, I pray,*

*Tra la la la la la lu la la la, tra la la la la la la la! O Gre-tel dear, O sis-ter dear, Your stocking has a hole! O Hän-sel dear, O bro-ther dear, D'you*

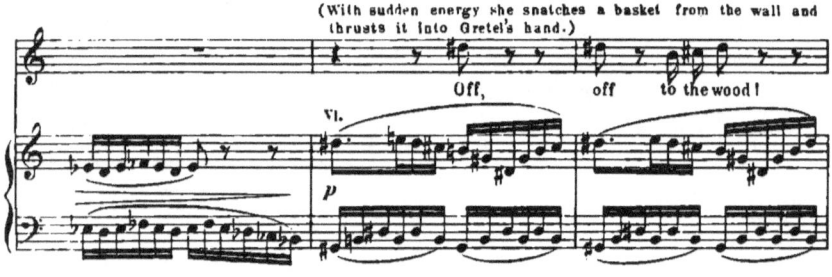

## Scene III.

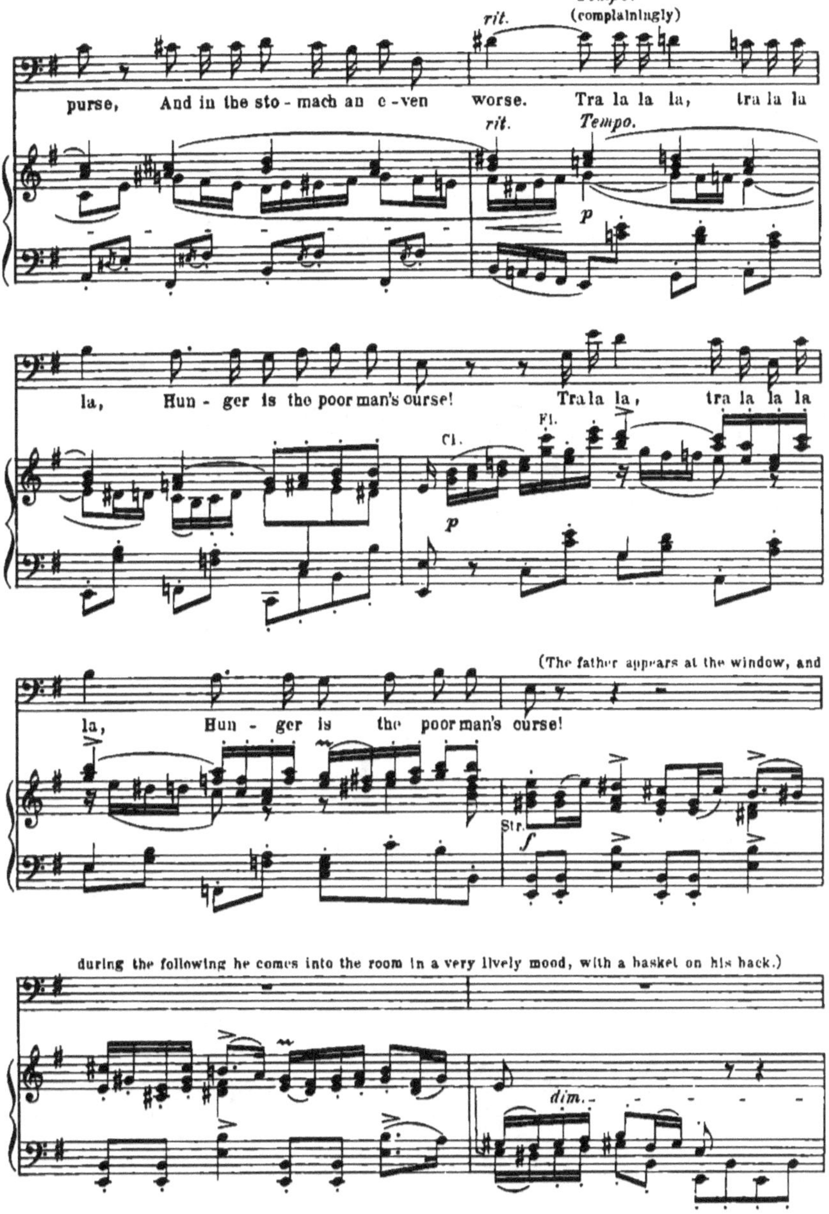

rit.
Tempo.
(complainingly)
purse, And in the sto - mach an e - ven worse. Tra la la la, tra la la
rit.
Tempo.
p
la, Hun - ger is the poor man's curse! Tra la la, tra la la la
Cl.
Fl.
p
(The father appears at the window, and
la, Hun - ger is the poor man's curse!
Str.
f
during the following he comes into the room in a very lively mood, with a basket on his back.)
dim.

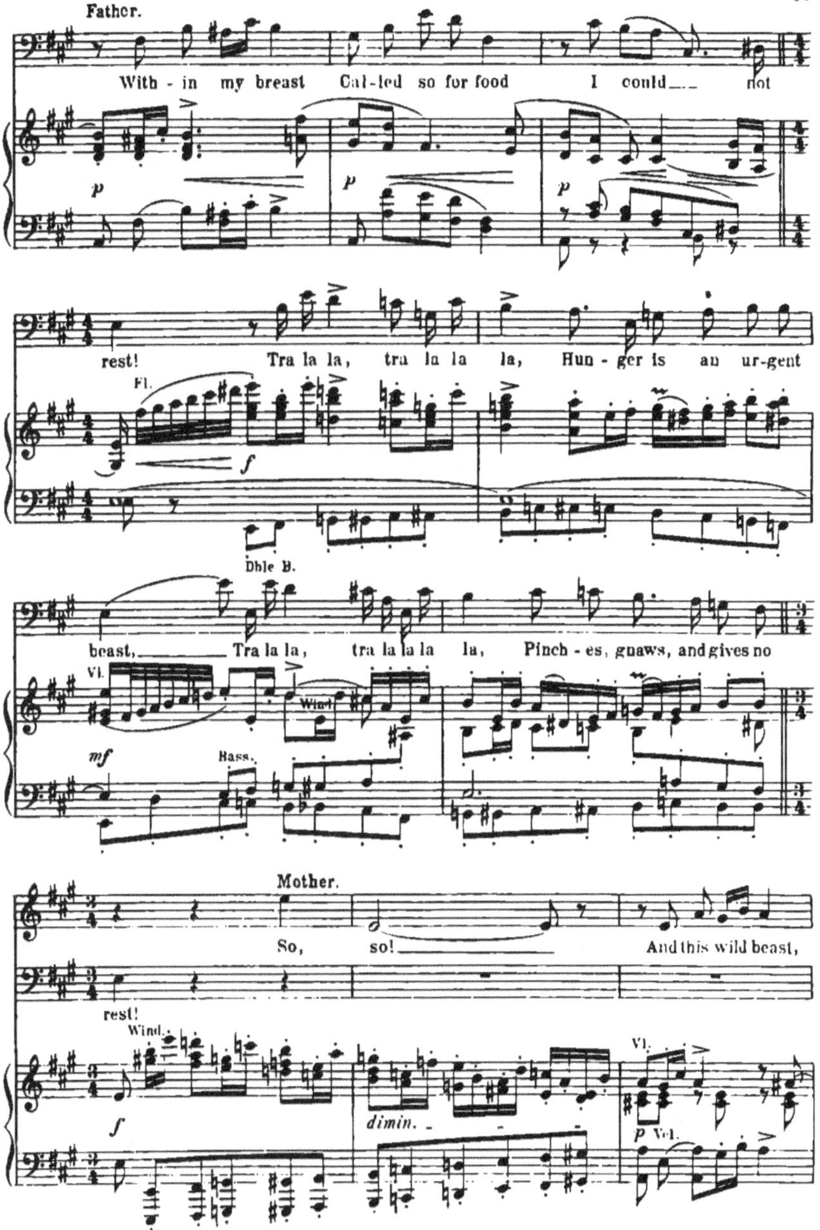
Father.
With - in my breast Cal - led so for food I could ___ not
p
p
p
rest! Tra la la, tra la la la, Hun - ger is an ur - gent
Fl.
f
Dble B.
beast, ___ Tra la la, tra la la la la, Pinch - es, gnaws, and gives no
Vl.
Wind
mf
Bass.
Mother.
So, so! ___ And this wild beast,
rest!
Wind.
f
dimin.
Vl.
p Vl.

You gave him a feast, He's had his fill, To say the least!
Father.
Well yes!
Hm! it was a love-ly day... don't you think so, dear wife?
Cl.
p
f
dimin.
(Pushing him angrily from her.)
(Wants to kiss her) Have done! You have no troubles to bear, 'tis I must keep the house!
Fl.
Bass.
Well, well!
cresc.

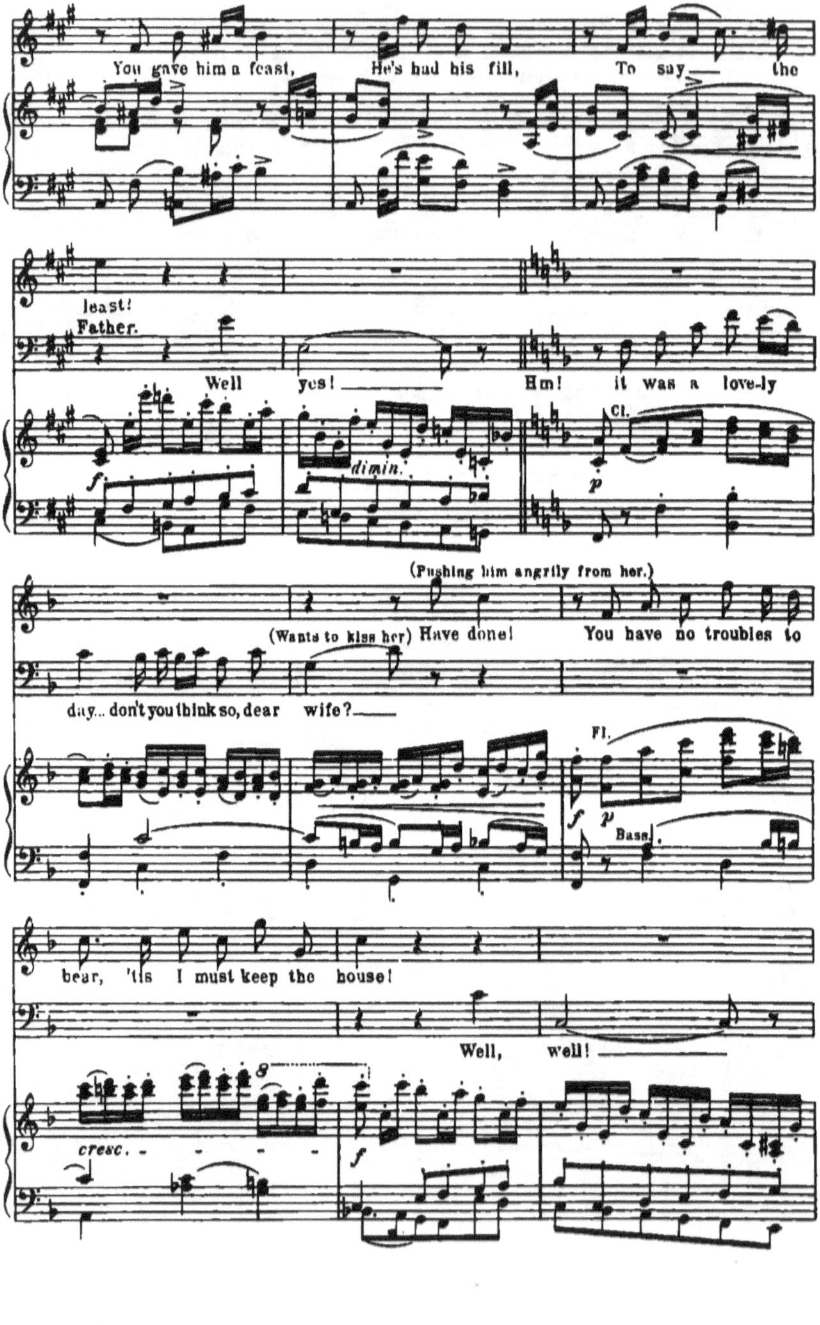

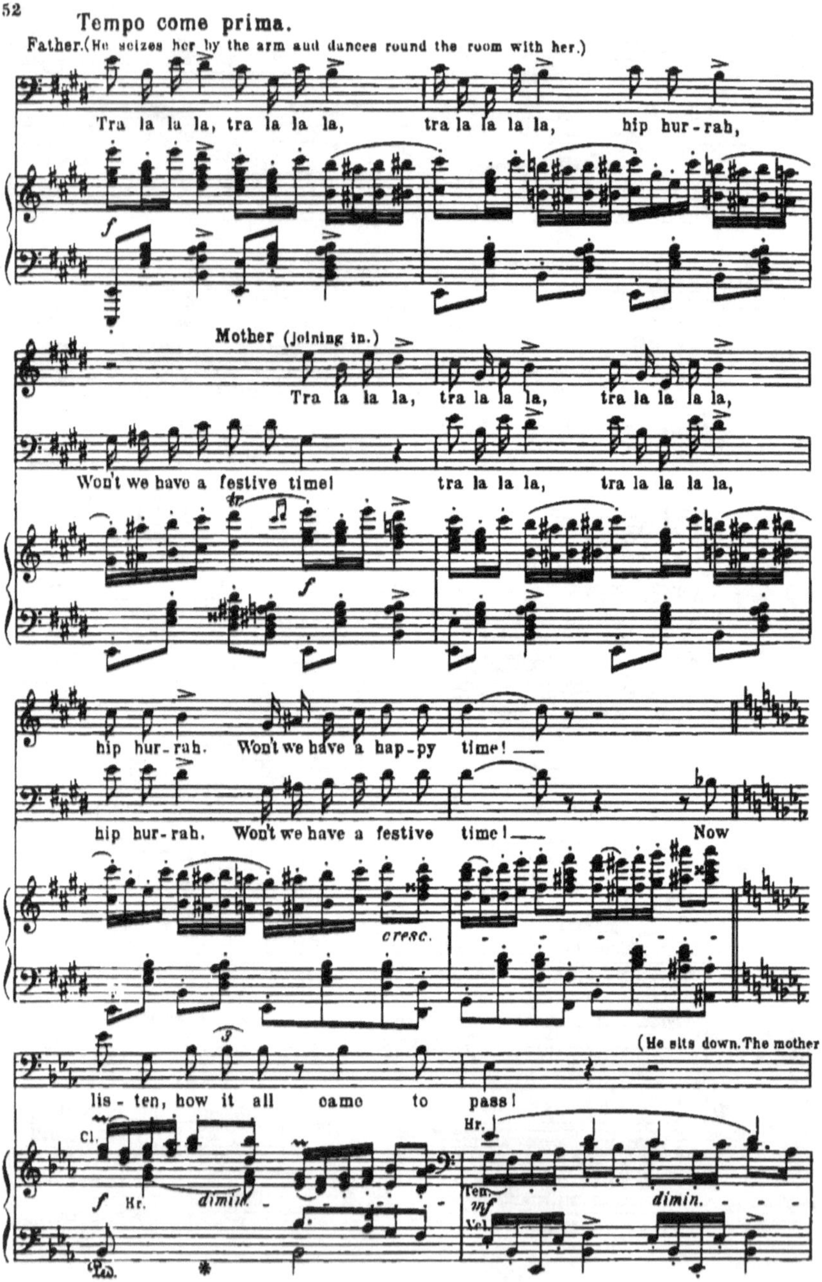
Tempo come prima.
Father. (He seizes her by the arm and dances round the room with her.)
Tra la la la, tra la la la, tra la la la la, hip hur-rah,
f
Mother (Joining in.)
Tra la la la, tra la la la, tra la la la la,
Won't we have a festive time! tra la la la, tra la la la la,
tr.
f
hip hur-rah. Won't we have a hap-py time! —
hip hur-rah. Won't we have a festive time! — Now
cresc.
(He sits down. The mother
lis-ten, how it all came to pass!
Cl.
Hr.
f Hr. dimin.
Ten.
mf
Vel.
dimin.
Ped.
*

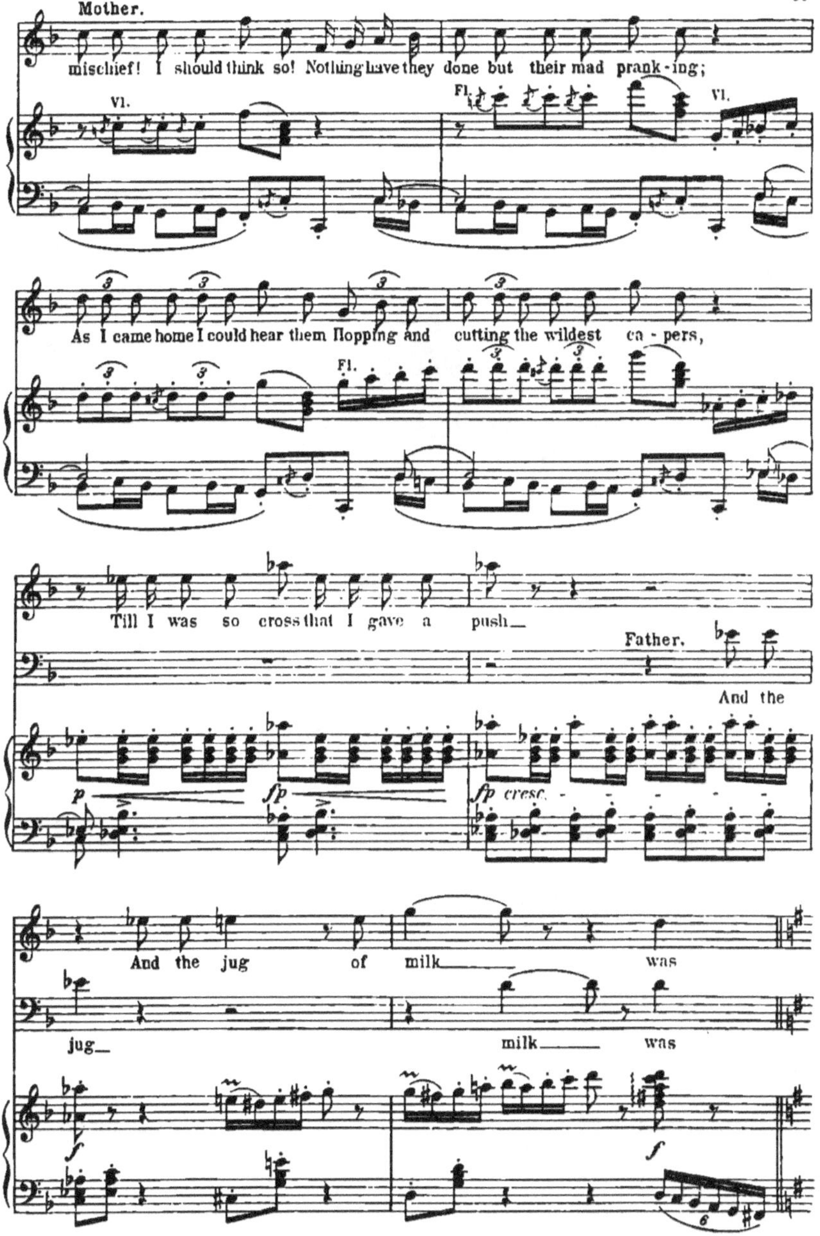
Mother.
mischief! I should think so! Nothing have they done but their mad prank-ing;
Vl.
Fl.
Vl.
As I came home I could hear them flopping and cutting the wildest ca-pers,
Fl.
Till I was so cross that I gave a push
Father.
And the
p
fp
fp cresc.
And the jug of milk was
jug milk was
f
f

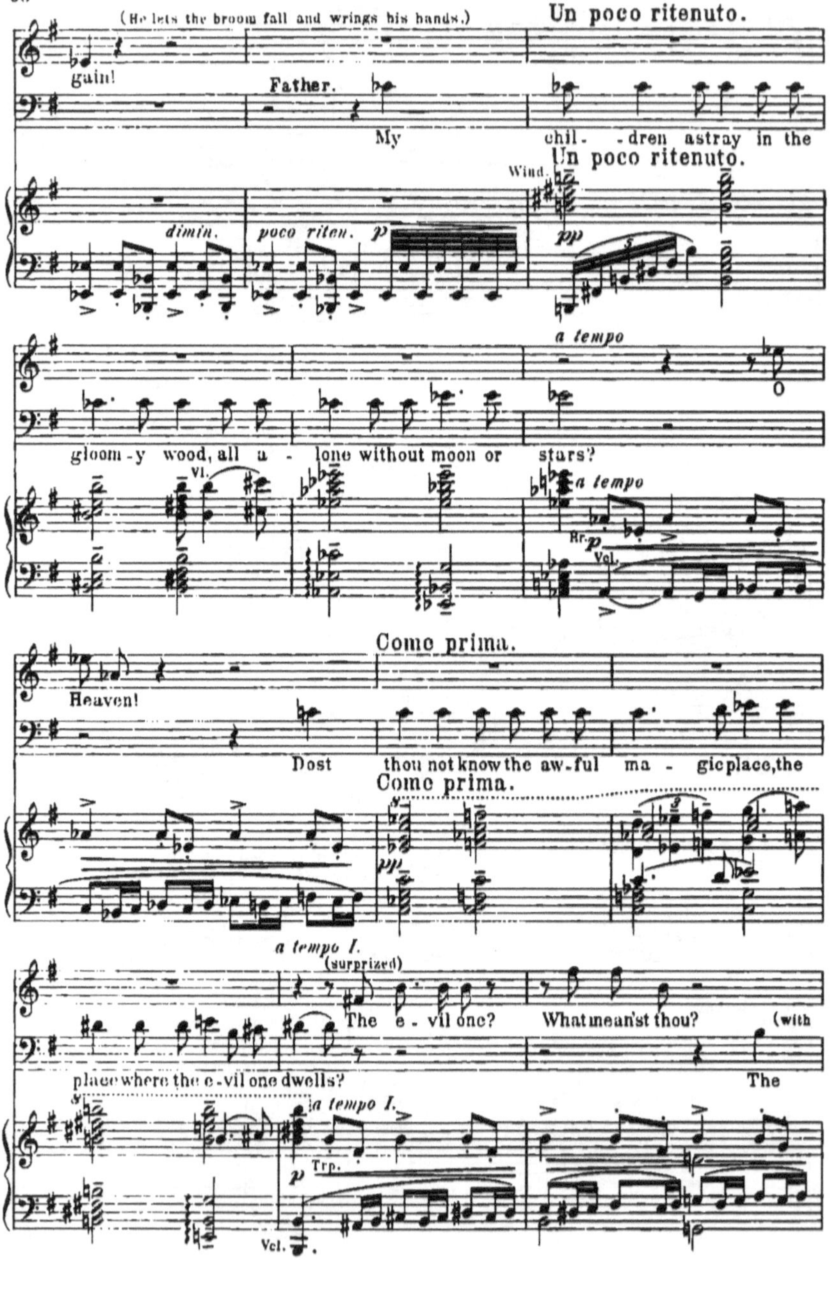
(He lets the broom fall and wrings his hands.)
Un poco ritenuto.
gain!
Father.
My children astray in the
Un poco ritenuto.
Wind.
dimin.
poco riten.
p
pp
a tempo
O
gloom-y wood, all a - lone without moon or stars?
Vl.
a tempo
Hr.
p
Vcl.
Heaven!
Come prima.
Dost thou not know the aw-ful ma - gic place, the
Come prima.
pp
a tempo I.
(surprized)
The e - vil one? What mean'st thou?
(with
place where the e-vil one dwells?
The
a tempo I.
Trp.
p
Vcl.

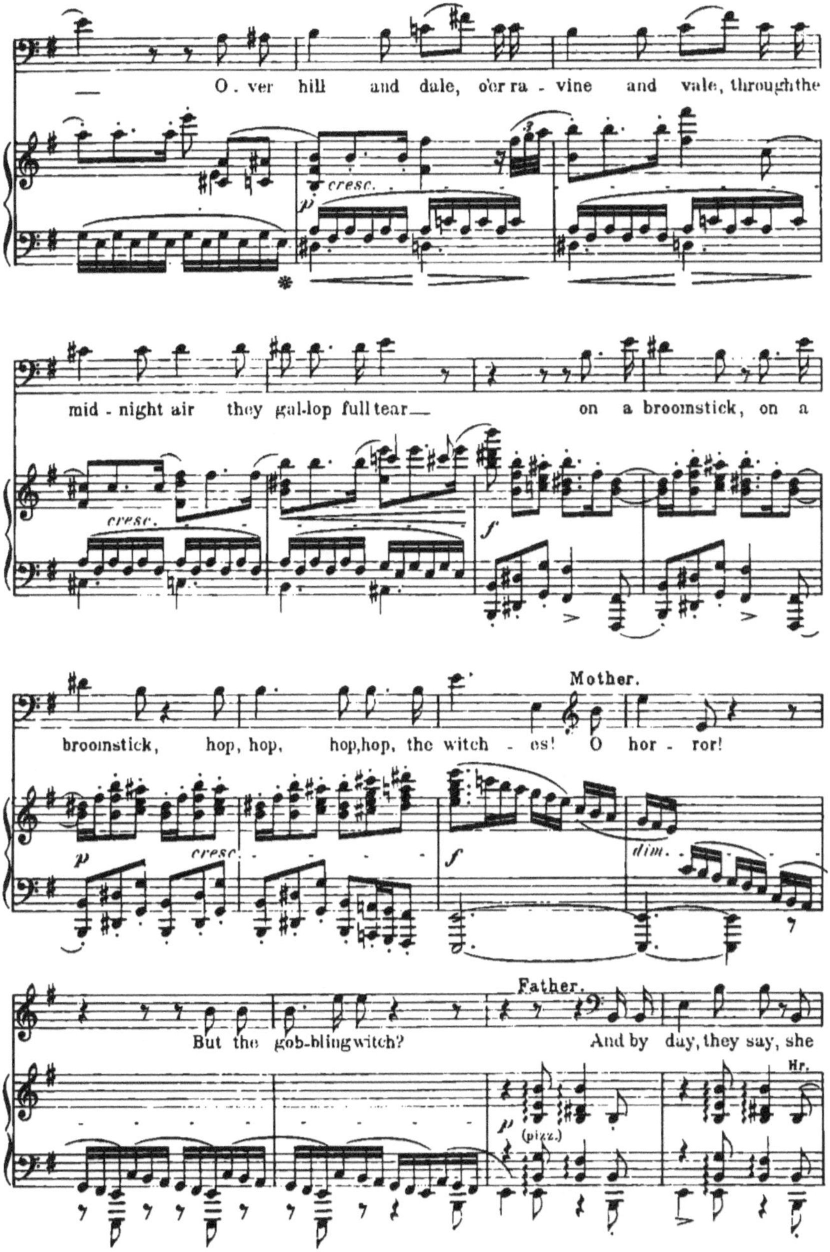
O.ver hill and dale, o'er ra - vine and vale, through the
cresc.
p
mid - night air they gal-lop full tear —
on a broomstick, on a
cresc.
f
broomstick, hop, hop, hop, hop, the witch - es!
Mother.
O hor - ror!
p
cresc.
f
dim.
But the gob-bling witch?
Father.
And by day, they say, she
p
(pizz.)
Hr.

# The Witches' Ride.
**Prelude to second Act.**

(The curtain rises.)
**Molto tranquillo.** (The middle of the forest. In the background is the "Ilsenstein", thickly surrounded by fir-trees. On the right is a large fir-tree, under which Gretel is sitting on a mossy tree-trunk, and making a garland of wild roses. By her side lies a nosegay of flowers. Amongst the bushes on the left is Hänsel, looking for strawberries. Sunset.)

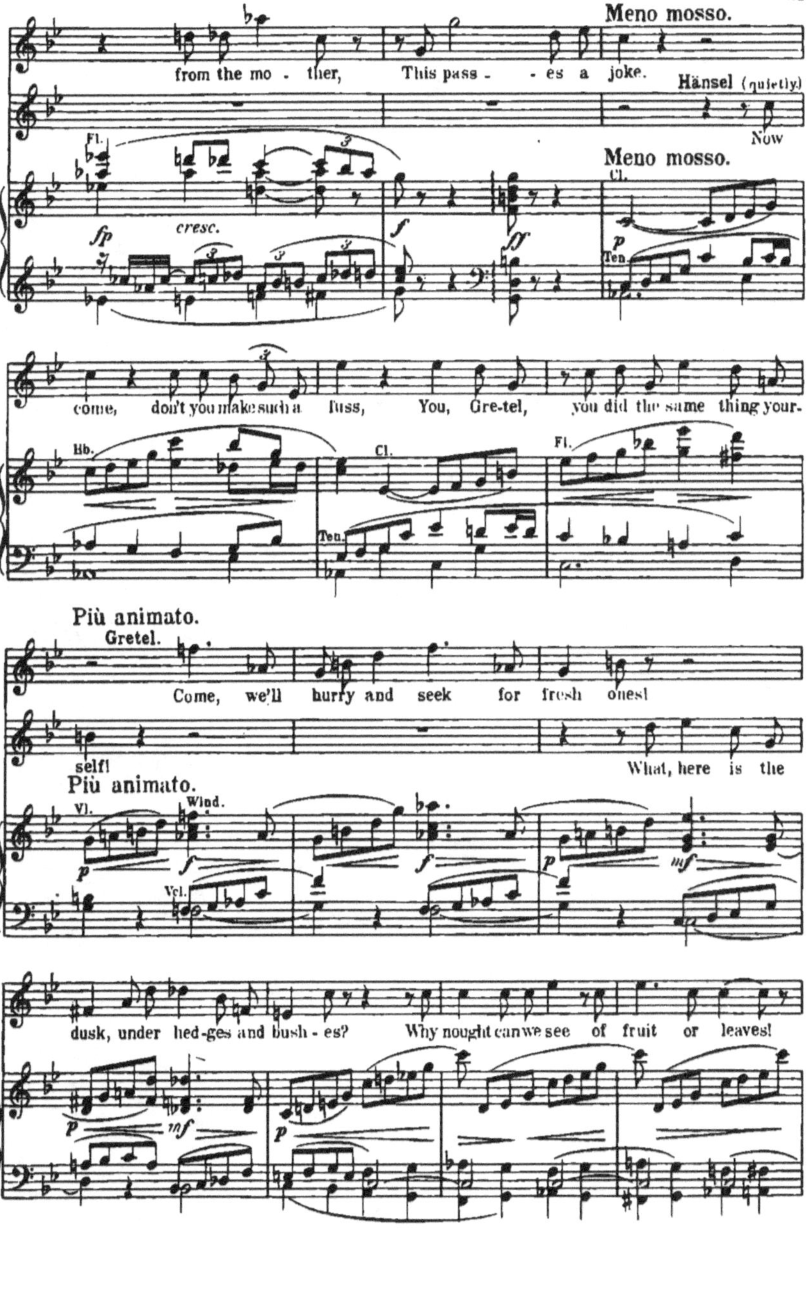
Meno mosso.
from the mo - ther, This pass - - es a joke.
Hänsel (quietly.)
Now
Fl.
cresc.
Meno mosso.
Cl.
Ten.
come, don't you make such a fuss, You, Gre-tel, you did the same thing your-
Hb.
Cl.
Fl.
Ten.
Più animato.
Gretel.
Come, we'll hurry and seek for fresh ones!
self!
What, here is the
Più animato.
Vl.
Wind.
Vcl.
dusk, under hed-ges and bush - es? Why nought can we see of fruit or leaves!

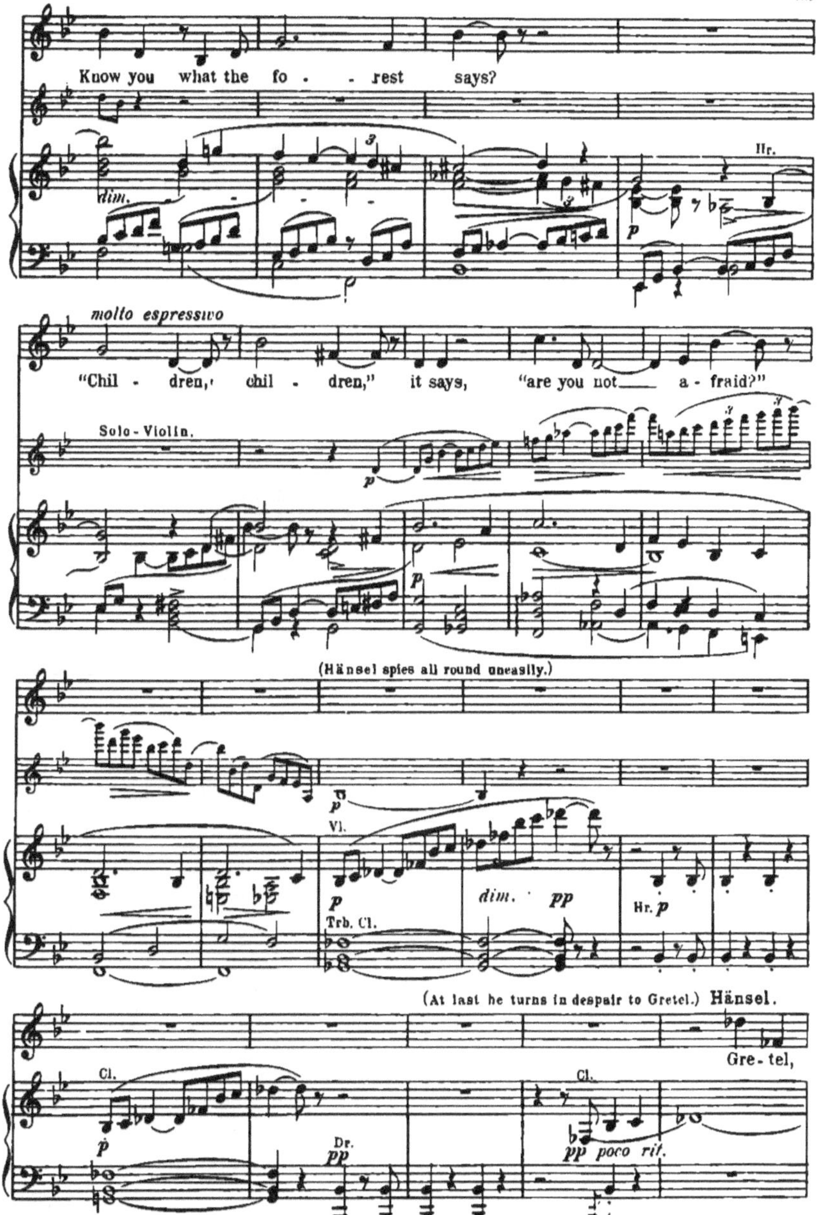

Know you what the fo - - rest says?
dim.
Hr.
p
molto espressivo
"Chil - dren," chil - dren," it says, "are you not a - fraid?"
Solo-Violin.
p
(Hänsel spies all round uneasily.)
Vl.
p
dim. pp
Trb. Cl.
Hr. p
(At last he turns in despair to Gretel.) Hänsel.
Gre - tel,
Cl.
p
Dr.
pp
pp poco rit.

## Scene II.

**Moderato.**

suddenly breaks through the mist, which forthwith rolls itself together into the form of a staircase vanishing in perspective in the middle of the stage.)

## Scene III.

### Pantomime.

(Fourteen angels, in light floating garments, pass down the staircase two and two, at

intervals, while it is getting gradually lighter. The angels place themselves, according to

98 *(The remaining angels now join hands and dance a stately dance around the group.)*

**Tempo moderato.**

# Third Act.
## The Witch's House.

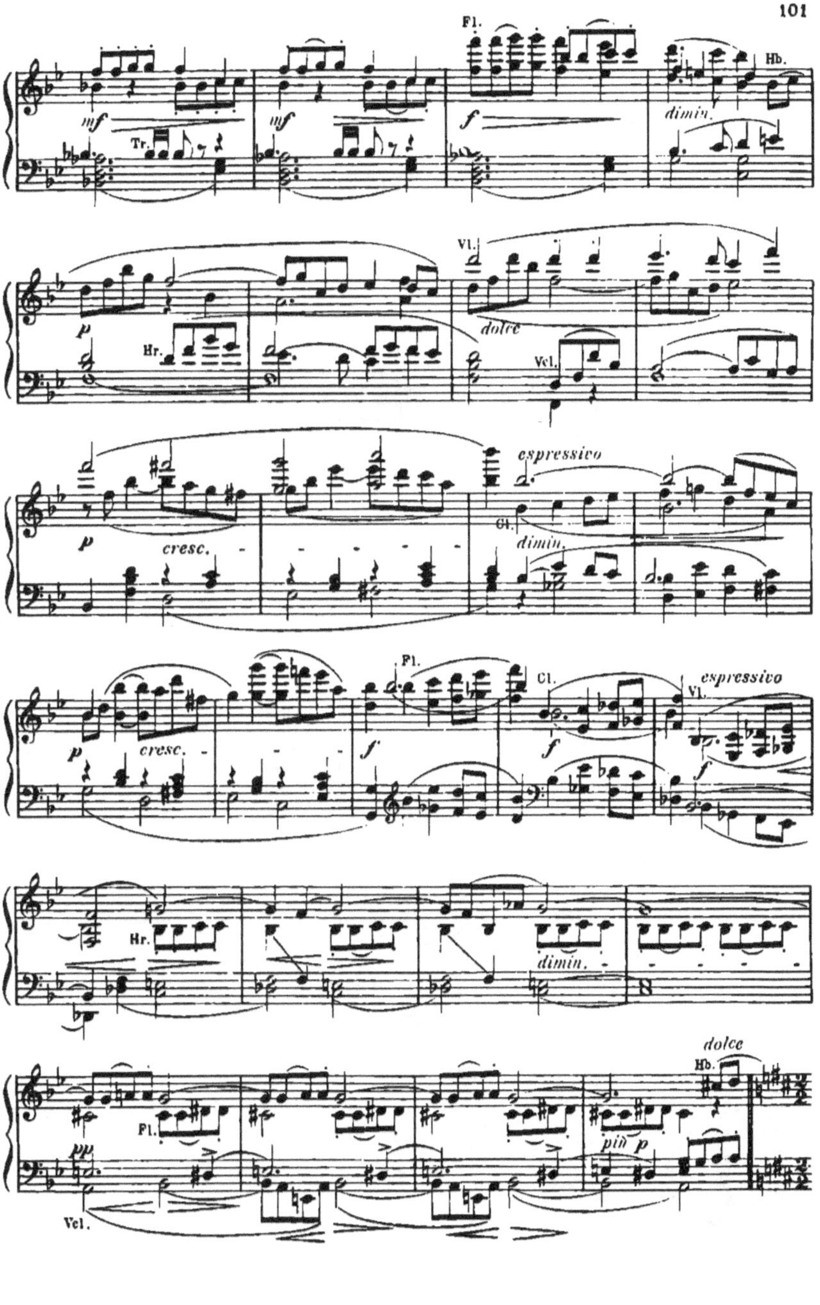
Fl.
Hb.
mf
Tr.
f
dimin.
Vl.
p
Hr.
dolce
Vcl.
espressivo
cresc.
Cl.
dimin.
Fl.
Cl.
espressivo
Vl.
f
Hr.
dimin.
dolce
Hb.
pp
Fl.
più p
Vcl.

## Scene I.

103

(Scene the same as at the end of Act II. The background is still hidden in mist, which gradually rises during the following. The angels have vanished. Morning is breaking. The Dew-Fairy steps forward and shakes dewdrops from a blue-bell over the sleeping children.)

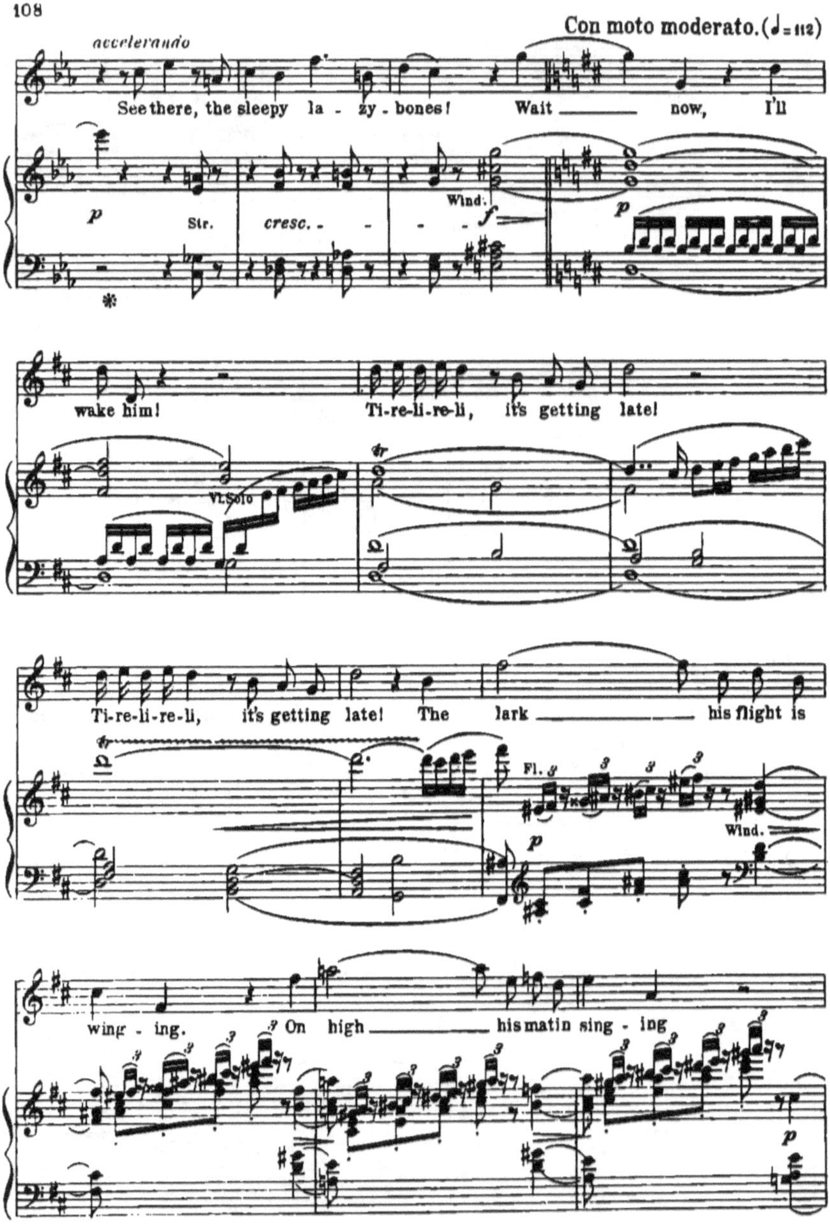
Con moto moderato. (♩ = 112)
accelerando
See there, the sleepy la - zy - bones! Wait now, I'll
p
Str.
cresc.
Wind.
f
p
wake him! Ti-re-li-re-li, it's getting late!
Vl. Solo
Ti-re-li-re-li, it's getting late! The lark his flight is
Fl.
Wind.
p
wing - ing. On high his matin sing - ing
p

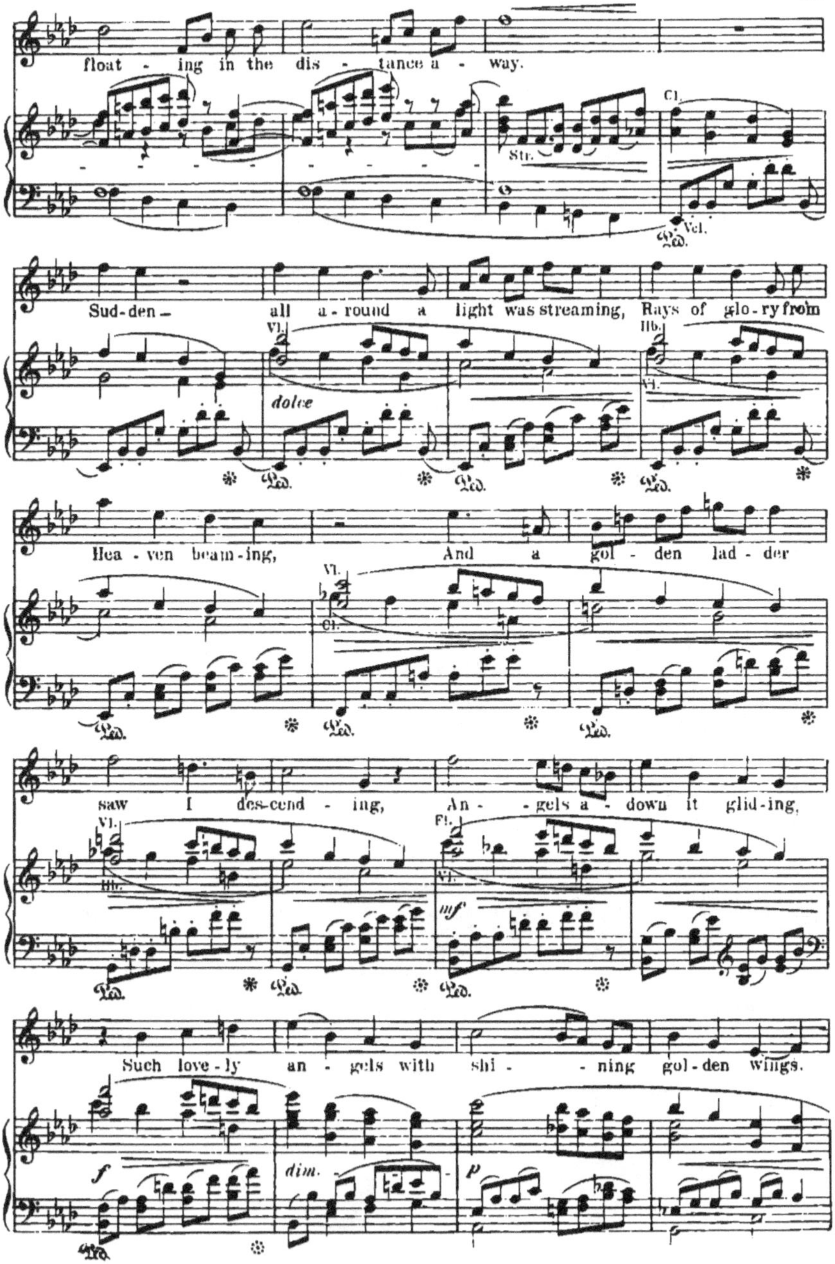
float - ing in the dis - tance a - way.
Cl.
Str.
Vel.
Sud-den— all a-round a light was streaming, Rays of glo-ry from
Vl.
Hb.
dolce
Hea-ven beam-ing, And a gol - den lad - der
Vl.
Cl.
saw I des-cend - ing, An - gels a - down it glid-ing,
Vl.
Hb.
Fl.
mf
Such love-ly an - gels with shi - - ning gol-den wings.
f
dim.
p

## Scene II.

(He turns towards the background: at this moment the last remains of the mist clear away. In place of the fir-trees is seen the Witch's House at the Ilsenstein, shining in the rays of the rising sun. A little distance off, to the left, is an oven; opposite this, on the right, a large cage, both joined to the witch's house by a fence of gingerbread figures.)

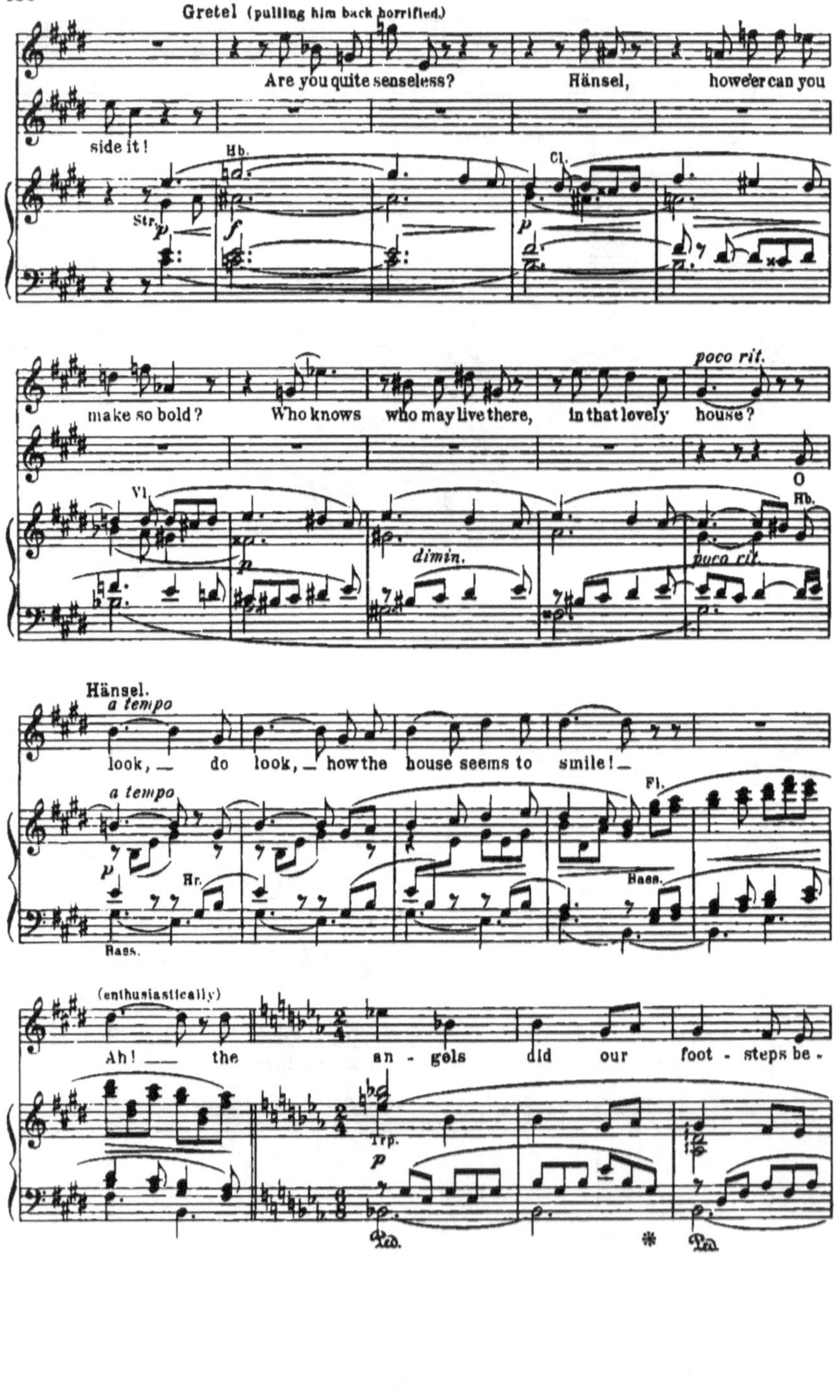
Gretel (pulling him back horrified.)
Are you quite senseless? Hänsel, howe'er can you
side it!
Hb.
Cl.
Str.
make so bold? Who knows who may live there, in that lovely house?
poco rit.
O
Vl.
Hb.
dimin.
poco rit.
Hänsel.
a tempo
look, — do look, — how the house seems to smile! —
a tempo
Fl.
Hr.
Bass.
Bass.
(enthusiastically)
Ah! — the an - gels did our foot - steps be -
Trp.

## Scene III.

138

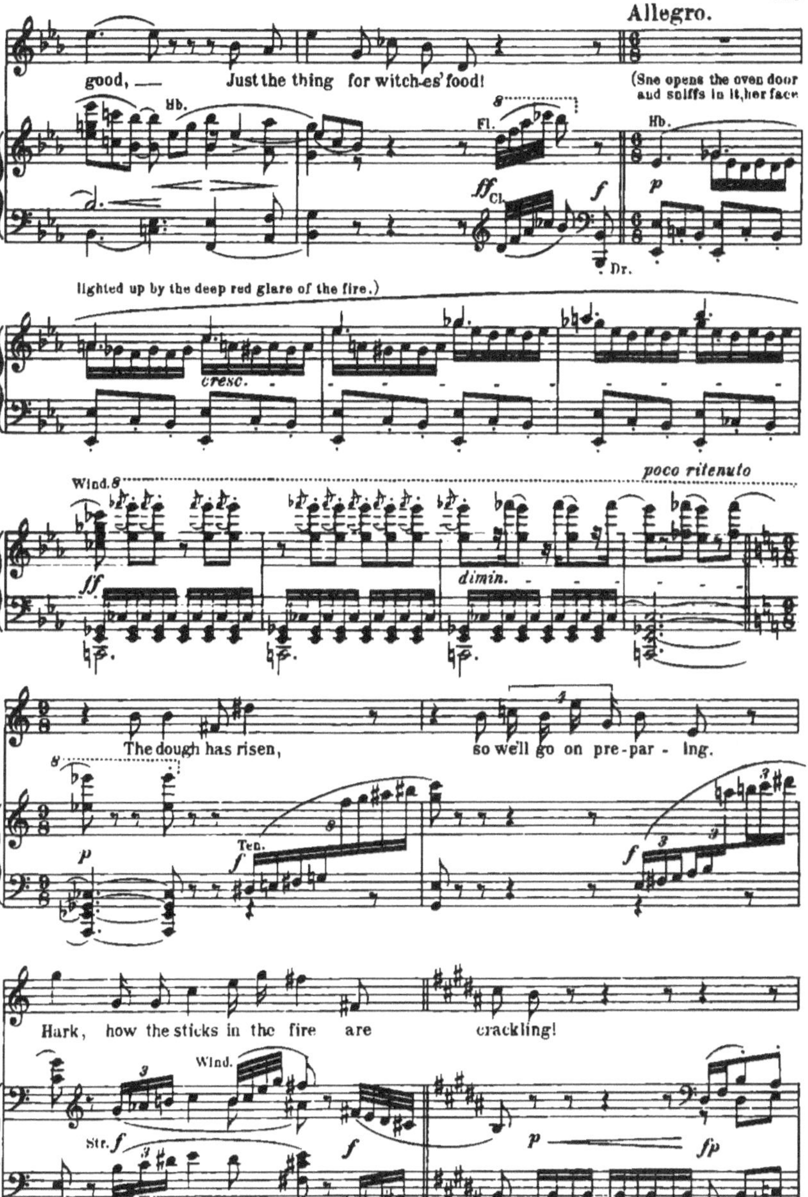
Allegro.
good, — Just the thing for witch-es' food!
(She opens the oven door and sniffs in it, her face lighted up by the deep red glare of the fire.)
Hb.
Fl.
ff
Cl.
f
p
Dr.
cresc.
Wind.
ff
dimin.
poco ritenuto
The dough has risen, so we'll go on pre-par-ing.
Ten.
Hark, how the sticks in the fire are crackling!
Str.
fp

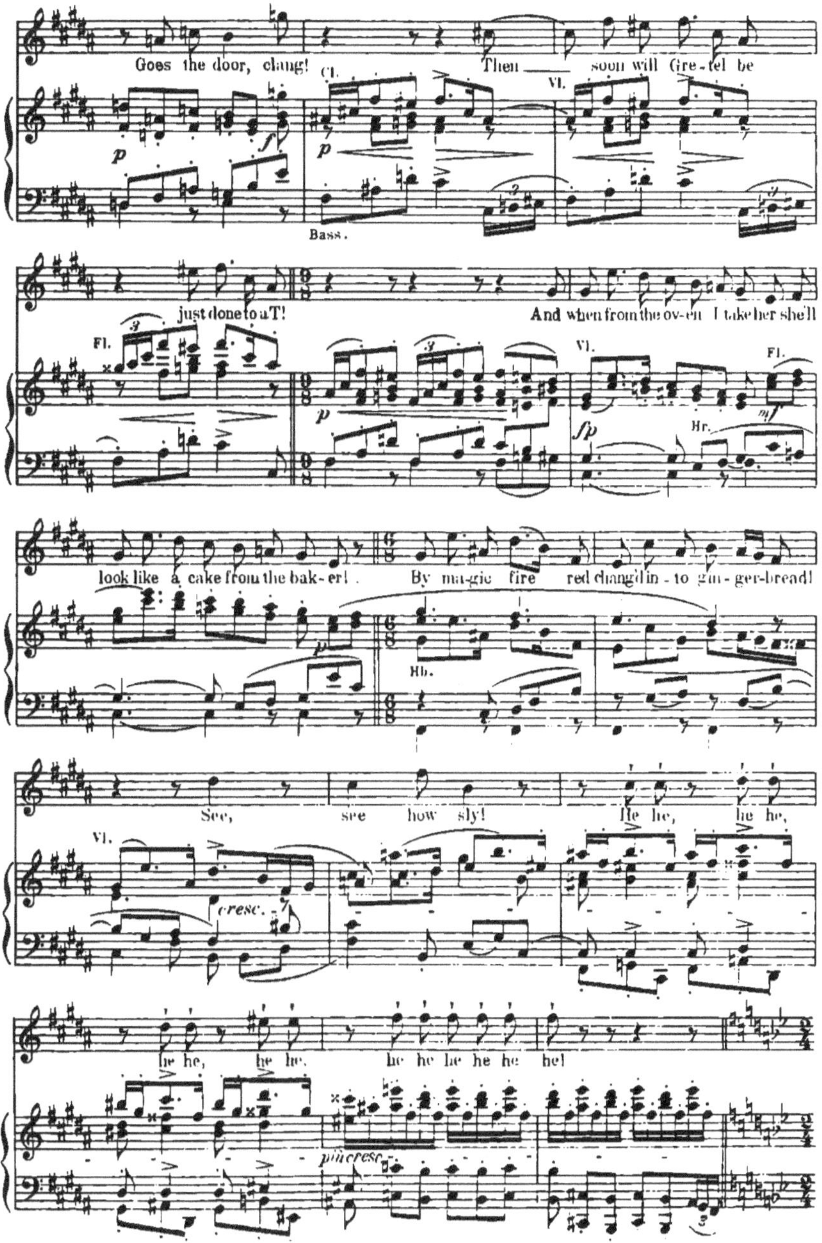
Goes the door, clang! Then soon will Gre-tel be
Cl.
Vl.
Bass.
just done to a T! And when from the ov-en I take her she'll
Fl.
Vl.
Hr.
look like a cake from the bak-er! By ma-gic fire red chang'd in-to gin-ger-bread!
Hb.
See, see how sly! He he, he he,
Vl.
cresc.
he he, he he, he he he he he he!
più cresc.

## L'istesso tempo. ($\flat = \flat$)

*(In her wild delight she seizes a broomstick and begins to ride upon it.)*

So hop, hop, hop, gal-lop, lop, lop! My broom-stick nag, come do not lag!

*(She rides excitedly round on the broomstick.)*

At dawn of day I ride a-way, Am

*(She rides again; Gretel meanwhile is watching at the window.)*

here and there and ev'-ry-where!

At mid-night hour, when none can know, to join the witch-es' dance I go!

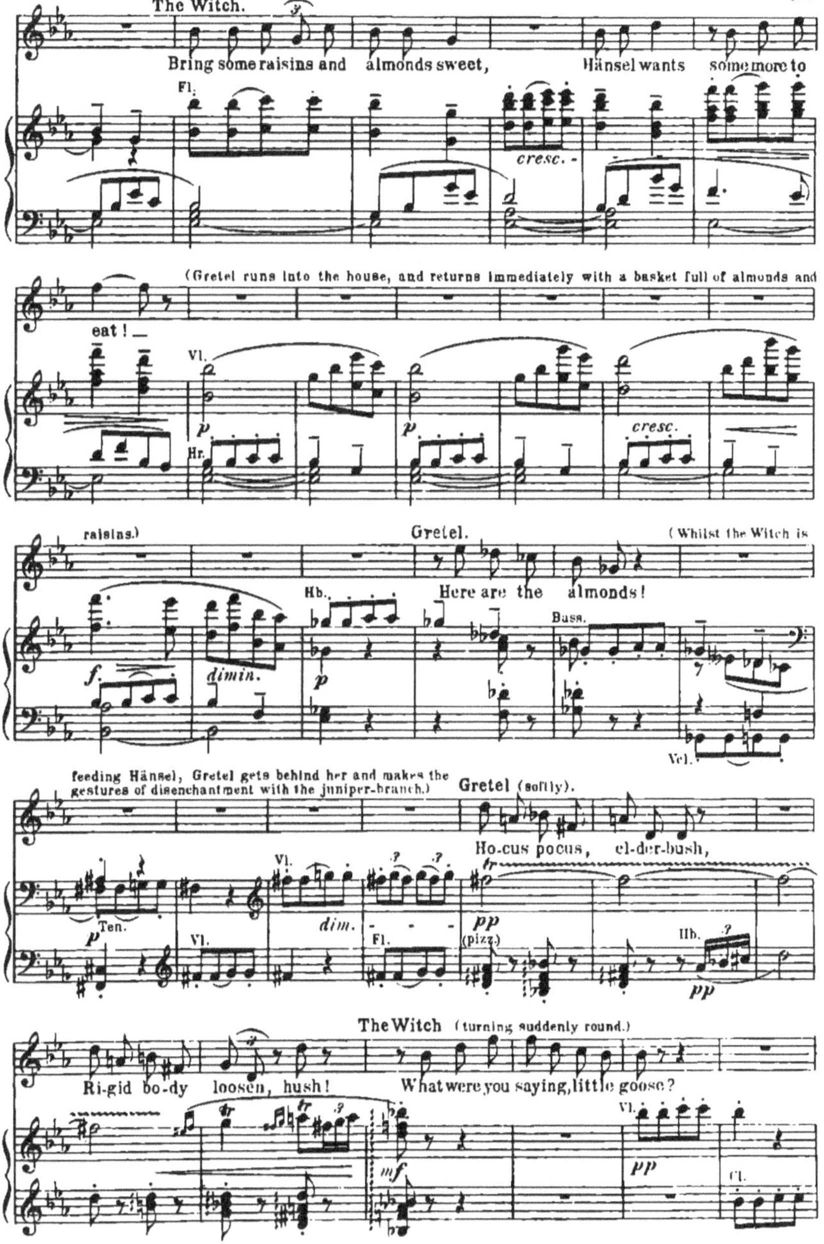
The Witch.
Bring some raisins and almonds sweet, Hänsel wants some more to eat! __
Fl.
cresc.
(Gretel runs into the house, and returns immediately with a basket full of almonds and raisins.)
Vl.
p
Hr.
cresc.
f
dimin.
Hb.
Gretel.
Here are the almonds!
Bass.
(Whilst the Witch is feeding Hänsel, Gretel gets behind her and makes the gestures of disenchantment with the juniper-branch.)
Vcl.
Ten.
Vl.
dim.
Fl.
Gretel (softly).
Hocus pocus, elder-bush,
pp
(pizz.)
Hb.
Rigid body loosen, hush!
The Witch (turning suddenly round.)
What were you saying, little goose?
mf
Vl.
Cl.

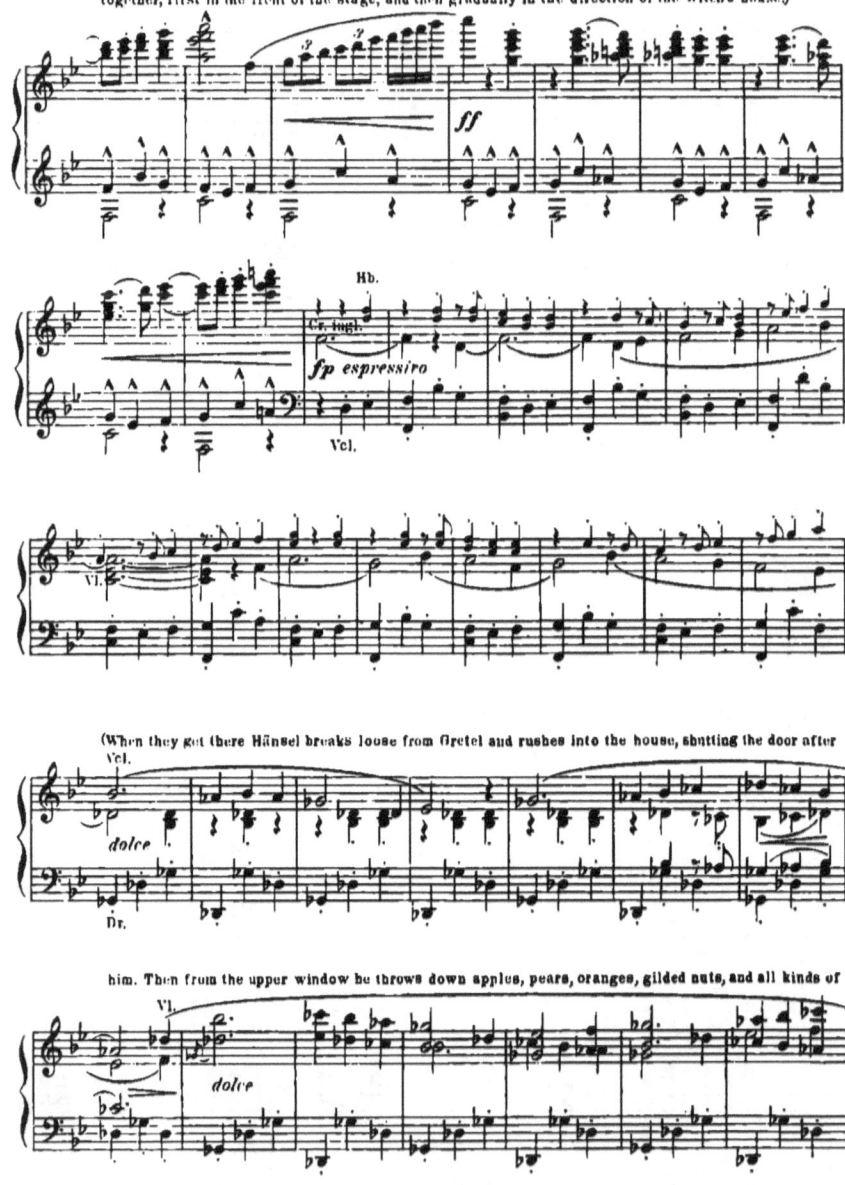

(Hänsel and Gretel, who in their terror let their sweetmeats all fall down, hurry towards the oven startled, and stand there motionless. Their astonishment increases when

they become aware of a troop of children around them, whose disguise of cakes has fallen from them.)

Gretel. (spoken) There, see those little children dear,
Hänsel. (spoken) I wonder how they all came here!

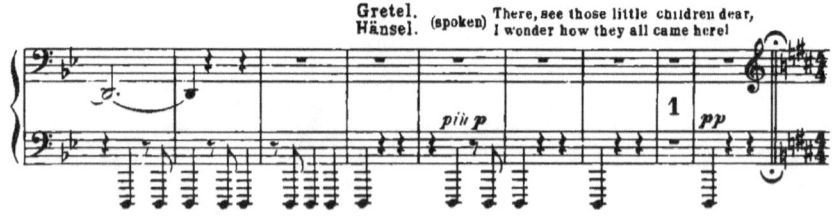

(She caresses the nearest child, who opens its eyes and smiles.)

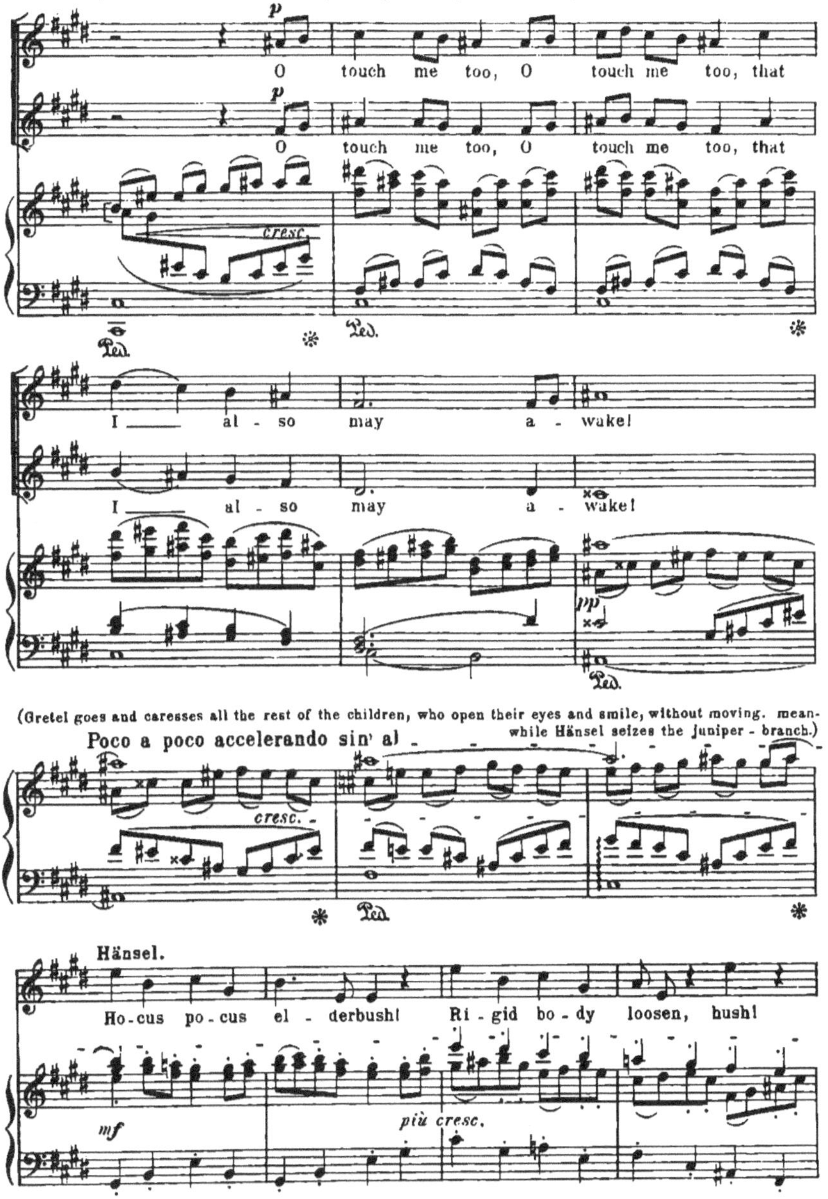
p
O touch me too, O touch me too, that
p
O touch me too, O touch me too, that
cresc.
I ___ al - so may a - wake!
I ___ al - so may a - wake!
pp
(Gretel goes and caresses all the rest of the children, who open their eyes and smile, without moving. meanwhile Hänsel seizes the juniper - branch.)
Poco a poco accelerando sin' al
cresc.
Hänsel.
Ho-cus po-cus el - derbush! Ri - gid bo - dy loosen, hush!
mf
più cresc.

www.ingramcontent.com/pod-product-compliance
Lightning Source LLC
Chambersburg PA
CBHW020254170426
43202CB00008B/358